Published by Willowisp Press, Inc.
401 East Wilson Bridge Road
Worthington, Ohio 43085

Printed in the U.S.A.

10   9   8   7   6   5   4   3   2   1

ISBN 0-87406-410-4

Designed and produced by
N.W. Books, 70 Old Compton Street, London W1V 5PA

FINDING OUT ABOUT
LIONS & TIGERS

By Kate Petty

Illustrated by
Tessa Barwick

Indian tiger

lion

Big cats

The lion and the tiger are the largest relations of the little cats we keep as pets. A male lion can be 10 feet long (including his tail). The biggest tigers are 13 feet long. Lions and tigers are wild, fierce creatures that have to kill other animals to stay alive.

More big cats

cheetah

cougar

leopard

jaguar

Lions in Africa

Most lions live on the open grasslands of Africa. They prey on the other animals that move across the plains in enormous herds. The lions are hard to see because their golden fur blends in with the sun-bleached grass.

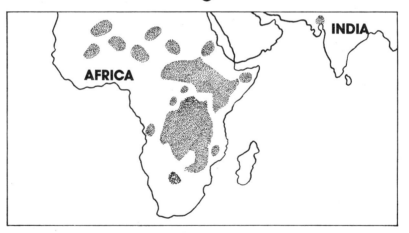

The shaded parts on the map show where lions live.

Lions live out in the open.

9

Tigers in Asia

Tigers live mainly in the jungles of northern India, but different kinds of tigers also live in many parts of Asia. Some even live in the snowy region of Siberia. Tigers are often found close to water.

The shaded parts on the map show where tigers live.

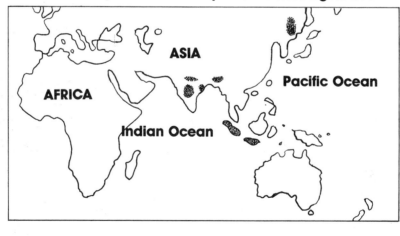

Tigers are good swimmers.

11

Indian tigers fighting

12

Keep away!

These tigers are fighting over hunting grounds. One male has entered an area that the other has claimed for his own. Like domestic tomcats, male lions and tigers mark out their territory by spraying it with their own particular scent. Intruders go in at their own risk.

A lion marks out its territory.

Weapons of a hunter

Lions and tigers have frightening sets of weapons – their teeth and claws! The four sharp, curved fangs stab the prey and hold it so the cat can eat it. The small front teeth can nip the skin. The back teeth are used for slicing. Lions and tigers have long claws. They keep them sharp by scratching on trees.

Cats can pull their claws in when they are not using them.

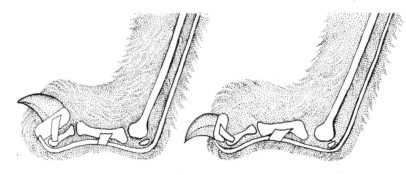

The lion shows its teeth.

14

15

Lions are the only cats that hunt together as a team.

Team work

Lions hunt by stalking and surprising their victims. The female lions do the hunting. They spread out and surround their victim, separating it from the herd. One female lion will move in and pounce on the victim. The others quickly join in the kill.

The lions' prey

zebra

wildebeest

small deer

warthog

Hunter in the shadows

Tigers hunt alone and at night. They creep up on their prey, padding silently on their powerful paws. Their stripes blend in with the shadowy trees, making them almost invisible. The tiger kills its victim quickly, knocking it to the ground and biting its neck.

The hunting tiger is easily hidden.

A tiger attacks a deer.

19

The adult male lions eat while the rest of the group wait for their turn.

The lion's share

The female lions caught the zebra, but the male lions eat the first share. When they have eaten their fill, the female lions and their young can move in for their share of the kill. An adult male lion needs to eat about 33 pounds of meat a week.

A pride of lions

Lions live together in groups called prides. The leader of the pride is an adult male. He defends the hunting ground and protects the females and cubs. As the male cubs grow older, they leave the pride.

The key shows how the female lions and cubs are related to female lion 1.
2 cousin; 3 half-sister; 4 daughter; 5 daughter; 6 mother; 7 son; 8 granddaughter. The male lions are the fathers of the cubs.

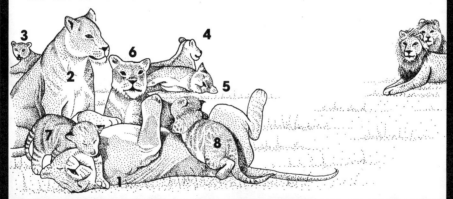

Mother tiger with young cubs

24

Rearing cubs

Tigers live alone. The father leaves the mother tiger to rear her two or three cubs by herself. The cubs drink milk from their mother for nine months. They are very dependent on her until they are about 18 months old. She has to teach them how to hunt.

Cubs playing hunting games

Rare beasts

Adult lions and tigers have no enemies in the wild, but their cubs need protection from other animals. It is human hunters and the loss of hunting ground that have made all the big cats endangered species.

An electronic collar helps scientists to keep track of the tiger and protect it.

This lion lives naturally in a reserve where people can observe it.   27

Identifying lions and tigers

This chart helps you to compare the sizes of lions and tigers. Tigers from different parts of the world vary in size and markings.

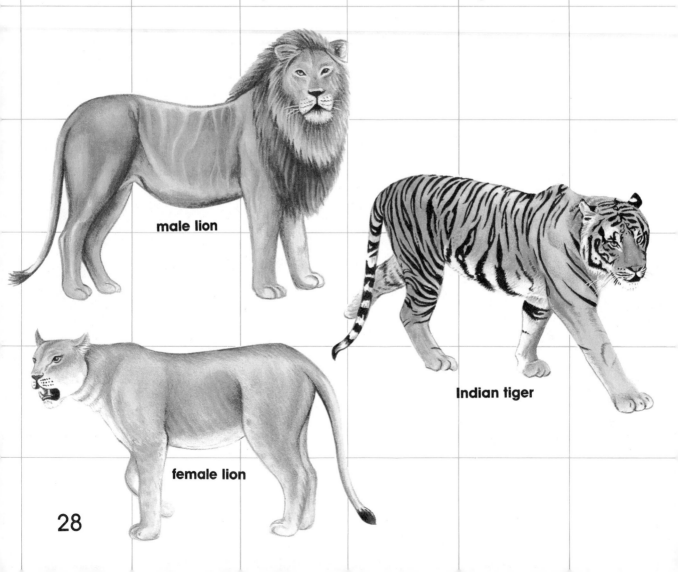

male lion

Indian tiger

female lion

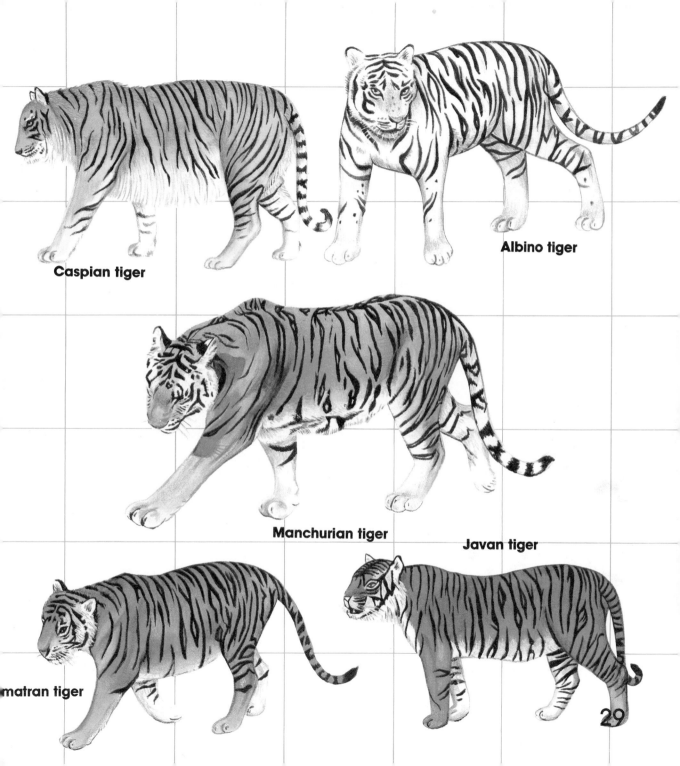

Caspian tiger

Albino tiger

Manchurian tiger

Javan tiger

matran tiger

29

Find the answers

Which is the biggest member of the cat family?

What are these cats called?

Can you name some other big cats?

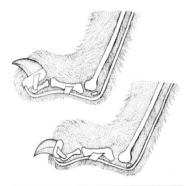

Why do cats need sharp claws?

How do they keep them sharp?

Can you describe a cat's teeth?

What are these animals called?

Where do they live?

How do the female lions hunt them?

Why do lions and tigers need to hide?

What sort of camouflage do lions have?

How does a tiger stay hidden?

How many cubs does a mother tiger usually have?

What does she have to teach them?

What are these cubs doing?

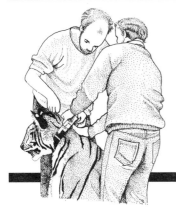

Why are lions and tigers under threat?

How can they be protected?

What is happening in this picture?

INDEX